This work is dedicated to the humans that are tired of being used as slaves.

The Roman Empire did not fall.
They just changed the name to the Roman Church.

YOU GOT A PROBLEM WITH THAT?
OFF WITH YOUR HEAD!!!

Introduction

This text contains material that you cannot un-read. Your thinking process will be permanently altered. Consider yourself warned. This text will release you from the Matrix and there is no way to get back inside. This is your final warning - DO NOT READ THIS BOOK!

How can we be so sure that history did in fact unfold as presented? We understand the world as it has been told to us by word of mouth or by subject matter experts. We place our faith in literary and biblical texts that have been edited over time. It is up to you to discern fact from fiction.

Everyone has their own agenda. What was the agenda of the writers of these enlightening literary works? If all of the books that have been burned were still on the shelf, what would the world look like today?

The world that we live in is riddled with countless mysteries and unanswered questions. From the most basic asks: *Why are we here?* to: *Where did the pyramids come from?* It doesn't seem that there are any definitive answers. Religions and cultures will attempt to provide explanations in their own dogmatic proclamations and yet they remain empty-handed of any concrete evidence. What people don't understand is that behind these questions lies a realm of myths and secrecies that are readily available to those who seek it; exceeding what any religion or theology can offer.

For most people, their thinking is done for them. There are countless outlets for the modern world to intrude upon, intercept and hijack an individual's thought process. From broadcast television, social media, world politics, you name it. Unless one anticipates and keeps a cautious eye open for being manipulated, one will remain susceptible to being conditioned by those who control what the masses are exposed to. The Media complex owns the minds of a large percentage of the population who will blindly follow them, as if they were being led by the Pied Piper.

The bottom line is that the governors of this planet have been manipulating humans for a very long time. Forever, actually. Each monarch, dictator, and institution has a hand in reprogramming your thought patterns. From birth, individuals are conditioned in a manner so that open discussion of *controversial* or *extreme* subjects are discouraged, shamed and even censored.

The effort to suppress free thinking is hidden behind the guise of good intentions. It is slowly becoming commonplace for governments and others to attack or prosecute individuals for *misinformation.* It's important to ask, where is the line drawn between keeping order and enacting blatant psychological warfare?

Why don't our indigenous natives generate technological innovations and achievements? Why are there tribes in certain spots of the Earth, untouched by any outside influence, that are still living as they did a thousand years ago? Why did they not progress at an equal pace alongside other human nations?

It is because a civilization is built upon the shoulders of one's forefathers. Civilizations do not spontaneously flourish. Native tribes can barely make a hut city. They certainly don't start cutting 2 million pound stones of granite to lay foundations for megalithic structures such as the Temple of Jupiter or the Temple Mount.

There are three of these 2-million-pound blocks in the foundation of the Temple of Jupiter. This one cracked so they left it at the quarry.

Do you really think that the existence of human civilization on Earth goes back only about 6,000 years? Does it sound reasonable that humans evolved from Neanderthals who lack basic understanding of their own mortality, to piloting space shuttles to the moon in such a short time?

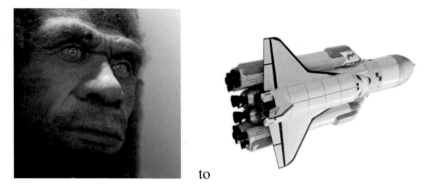

to

I would dare say that this is exponentially faster than we would typically expect an evolutionary process to unfold.

This aqueduct was built with advanced engineering principles. Greatly ahead of its time.

Prologue

In 1946, a massive cache of ancient manuscripts were found in caves near the dead sea. These became known as the "Dead Sea Scrolls". I have studied various forms of this material for the past 15 years. I have examined historical documents, religious texts as well as countless historical facts. These texts have led me to a number of obvious realizations. There are texts known as *forbidden knowledge* in most cultures. Most have been burned. If you explore them, you will find that they all lead to extraterrestrial origins.

Recent research has revealed that humans are composed of between 1% and 4% of the Neanderthal's DNA. The part that was not mentioned was that there are humans with 0% Neanderthal DNA in them. This is the Roman *race*. (The other 96%)

These *pureblood* humans are the aliens who came to Earth and created Earthling humans through genetic manipulation. The Romans mixed their DNA with Neanderthals to create a race of workers to satisfy their labor needs.

In anthropological circles, they would be called *the missing link*. You can find them in our historical records as *Ancient Romans and Greeks*. They appeared out of nowhere, enacted biblical scale changes to humanity and then disappeared as mysteriously as they came.

Thoughtfully and critically consider the facts, they actually make far more logical sense than the stories you have been indoctrinated to believe.

History is written and rewritten by the victor. The Romans have erased and revised Earthly history to suit their agenda. They continue this practice even today as books and monuments are removed. Free discourse is censored and self-anointed ultra-biased fact checkers have appeared on the scene to employ psychological warfare upon the masses. Political foes are imprisoned. *The Inclusive Bible* is the latest Bible translation where the writers have removed male pronouns and sexism.

Facts should remain facts and not subject to subverting by whoever is in power at the time. A fact never changes. Religion and history are not subjects to be modified and rewritten at the whims of a new leader.

Planetary Governor Klaus Schwab recently stated that we will not even recognize the Earth in a few years.

I. The Off-Worlders

The ancient cuneiform tablets have clearly detailed that an extraterrestrial lifeform came to Earth. They needed workers so they genetically modified the Neanderthals to produce the human race. They made themselves known to us as Gods. Since they were our creators, it is a fair assertion. (*Our Father who art in heaven. God created man in his own image* - sound familiar?)

Ancient Rome is ***EXACTLY*** what it looks like when a highly advanced space-faring race frontiers a new planet. The Roman race brought all of the various disciplines of a complex civilization with them. They did not ***invent*** anything (except humans).

You may call them what you wish: Martians, Angels, Atlanteans, GOD, Gods, Greeks, Anunaki, Aliens, Nefilim, Blue Eyed Devils, Nibiruans, Watchers, or whatever you like. For my purposes, I will refer to them as Romans (The Roman *race*). This text will discuss the real origin of Earthly humans and who created them.

Wotan (Germanic God Odin)

Long ago, the Roman *race* arrived on Earth to obtain gold. Their planet was suffering from an ecological disaster and they required gold for remediation. They sent ships to asteroids to obtain gold, but the ships never returned.

In a bold and desperate move, the Romans crossed the asteroid belt to come to Earth. Not only did this new world have gold, but more importantly it had vegetation, fish, animals, water and air.

They had intended to utilize a sluice mining technique to obtain the rare and precious mineral. Unfortunately, this did not prove to be a productive method. While seeking greater efficiency, they found significant gold deposits in the depths of the Earth. South Africa became the first mining location.

Gold - This is why they came.

753 BC to 476 AD is over 1250 years that the common worker Roman had control over their own dominion on Earth. This was the period in which the ***Roman race*** stood in the open and revealed themselves for what they truly were. How exactly did they manage to completely skip the native part of evolution and appear on the scene with such greatly advanced technology?

Some of the working class Romans had migrated to lands outside of the control of their Royal leaders. They revealed their advanced civilization's roots through the use of their complex technology and introduction of countless ***inventions***.

The Roman Royals are what we know in ancient history as the pantheon of Gods: Neptune, Jupiter, Mercury, Mars, and so on. Ancient Greeks are the same race. They had a similar pantheon, and a similar language. For the purposes of this text, they are the same: The Roman *race*.

Dionysius I of Syracuse

The Roman *civilization* **invented** an alphabet, numbering system, mathematics, philosophy, law, roads, dams, bridges, arches, buildings, concrete, military technology, medical technology, human power, animal power, water power, steam power, vending machines, automatic doors, gimbal, carts, block and tackle, polybolos, bridge building, steam ball, polyspastos, archimedes screw, etc...

The list of *inventions* and scientific disciplines for which Romans are responsible is endless. **All inventions, actually.**

These empirical geniuses didn't just appear out of nowhere. It's clear that the Romans originated from a place with a highly advanced level of education. As previously stated, a civilization is built on the shoulders of the man before him. It does not just appear. Nowhere else in history do spontaneous genius abilities simply appear out of thin air. Truly amazing how the Roman *civilization* managed to entirely skip the native phase of evolution.

The Roman *race* landed in Kuwait. They migrated up the Euphrates river and encircled the Mediterranean sea. They began as Sumerians, their offspring grew into Akkadians and Babylonians and so on. The mere existence of the white human on Earth is evolutionary lunacy on its face. White humans can't even tolerate sunlight.

II. Four Races

The Roman *race* are typically tall caucasians. The Romans were the *Race of the Masters* in de-facto terms because they possessed superior technology. They are the *Master Race* in terms of genetic purity because their blood had not yet been diluted with Neanderthal blood.

The Roman workers came to harvest the rare and precious mineral gold. It was required in order to save their planet from an atmospheric calamity. The sluice mining that was implemented did not provide the yields anticipated so they changed their plan to mine directly from the depths of the Earth. After enduring endless hardship and toil, the Roman workers revolted against their leaders and refused to work.

The leaders were in desperate need for gold as this was not a mission for conquest or wealth but for their very existence. As a proposed solution, the Royal Roman second prince, Yahweh, suggested to the Royal leadership council to combine Roman essence with Earthling hominids to grant them the intelligence to follow directions. After intense arguments and discussion, it was finally decided that a new worker would be created from the mixing of Roman and the Neanderthal blood. This stroke of genius redirected the course of Earthly history forever as it led to the creation of the **superior** Earthling human race. This new race would complete the hard labor for the Romans in the gold mines.

The Romans were successful in creating these new hybrid beings... except that they were sterile. After countless failures, desperate measures became necessary. Their immediate need for workers forced the science leaders to take dire actions. Yahweh and his half-sister Ninmah took the Hybrid Beings and transplanted sex glands from the Royal leaders into these Hybrids. This is commonly known today as Adam's rib being used to make Eve. When an ovary and a testicle were transplanted from the Roman Royals into the sterile Hybrids, they became fertile and were instructed to procreate with haste. This is where Mother Nature genetically combined in the womb the being that was mostly Roman (Hybrid Roman/Neanderthal) with a pure Roman (sex glands) to create a slight variation of themselves.

This combination was the creation of the Earthly human race. The Roman with 4% Neanderthal, or the Negro Human Race.

The medical symbol (Staff of Hermes) depicts *one being* rising out of the combination of the Hybrid and Roman chromosomes woven together.

These new fertile humans were the same as the royals in every way, except they were born with a foreskin and were physically superior. Roman males do not have a foreskin. The Negro humans were musclebound giants that were greatly superior to their forefathers. Romans considered humans to be abominations.

Facts indicate that every human heart pumps Royal Roman blood.

Nevertheless, this led to the enslavement of the humans by the Roman working class and the birth of racism. After some time passed, Yahweh mated with a Negro female. From this mating, the yellow human race was created. This was the birth of the 2% Neanderthal. More time passed, and there was a mating between Yahweh and a yellow human to create the white human race. This was the birth of the 1% Neanderthal.

Yahweh's promiscuity was legendary.

This new white human (Noah), his associates and family were spared during the great flood. A few of the other humans survived and were scattered about the Earth, floating until they found land on high ground. This is one of the ways humans were scattered about the Earth.

The great flood was caused by a cosmic event that could not be avoided. The Royal Roman first prince Muhammed ordered that no human be warned of the coming calamity so that all of the human abominations would be eradicated from the Earth. This would clean up the abominations once and for all. Muhammed had always been against the creation of the humans and was disgusted at all of the different levels of defiling one could inflict upon the Roman race by diluting it with the Neanderthal blood.

The Great Flood was the Great Reset I.

III. Domains

Royal Roman children would be granted their own domain and some humans to manipulate. The higher the ranking child, the more the Romans would dedicate resources to build that domain. Romans grew tribes of humans for their needs and desires to serve all of the Royal Romans. This is how the various Earthly religions, regions and countries were formed.

More and more domains sprouted up over the lands as the Royal leaders (Gods/Kings) had children and the Royal Roman children (more Gods/Kings) grew their nations. These nations were meant to be kept separate and distinct to avoid conflict.

These are the roots of all of the highly engineered ancient architecture around the world. The Roman race designed and constructed all of the ancient monuments, cities, temples and human colonies. (Temple of Jupiter, Giza Pyramid, Temple Mount, Barbegal mega factory, Easter Island, Nemi Tunnel, Temple of the Moon, Caesarea Harbor, Angkor Wat, Puma Punku, Hagia Sofia, Chichen Itza, Basilica Cistern, Nasca, Machu Picchu, Aqueducts and yes, even the Face on Mars).

Every one of those structures were designed and built by the Roman race (with some hard labor help from humans). Humans cannot engineer and erect these structures even today. Without Roman rule, humans would be natives.

The earliest major landing sites: Temple of Jupiter, Nazca, Temple Mount.
Temple Of Jupiter (survived the Great Flood)

Spaceship landing site at Nazca

Nazca was used when the great flood destroyed earlier sites. Temple Mount
and the Temple of Jupiter had structures built on top of them at later dates,
so they don't appear to be landing pads.

As long as the gold was flowing, nothing else really mattered except to try to keep everyone happy and working. The plight of the humans meant nothing. They were animals and abominations. Only Yahweh and his half-sister Ninmah cared about the humans because they were their offspring.

Yahweh's son Marduk was promised by his father that he would one day rule the Earth. This greatly fueled the young prince's ambition. Marduk began seizing power and started building his own launch tower. The Roman leadership council decided that this was unacceptable and obliterated the tower.

The Roman leaders felt that the Earthlings were becoming too organized and too powerful. So they took the humans, confounded their languages and dispersed them about the Earth. This is yet another way humans were populated about the various lands of the Earth. This event was depicted in the Roman Bible as the Tower of Babel. At this time the Romans and humans spoke one language. Latin. This is the root Romantic language and the mother tongue of the off-worlders. Many languages today stemmed from Latin roots. This is when they burned the Library of Alexandria.

Dispersing humans and creating languages was the Great Reset II

Romans had plenty of issues following orders amongst themselves. Some 200 of them came from the way-station on Mars to attend Marduk's wedding to the Earthling Sarpanit. After the wedding, they stole wives, generating the term *Fallen Angels*. Then they splintered away from their royal leaders and migrated to the area on and around the peninsulas (Greece-Italy) to create their own domains.

These are the groups you think of as *The Roman Empire and The Ancient Greeks*. They were unruly splinter groups.

The Romans were more warlike and the Greeks were more intellectually oriented. For this discussion, the Romans and the Greeks are the same, simply called Romans. They worshiped the Royal Roman pantheon: Mercury, Venus, Jupiter, etc... They presented the Royal Romans as gods to the humans so the Royals ignored them and let them run amok for a time.

The native Roman was born with armor, advanced weaponry and complex military tactics.

IV. Theology

At a point, plenty of gold was flowing to save the Roman home planet from their ecological disaster. Now it was becoming more of a plan to control and extort the humans on a long term basis. The extreme defiling of the humans was becoming less and less tolerated by the Royals.

Is that a Roman coming over the hill?

RUN FOR YOUR LIFE! YOU ARE ABOUT TO BECOME A SLAVE!

The Roman *empire's* Constantine rose to power. The Council of Nicaea was created to bring the entire planet under one Roman control. It was decided (by the Roman Royals) that the holy pantheon was outdated and there was a need to simplify all royal gods into one god named GOD. They plagiarized the Hebrew Bible, sterilized the pantheon into monotheistic terms and rewrote it in their own image (The Holy Roman Bible).

To solidify this new image, they set out to exterminate all Jews. Once accomplished, the Hebrew bible would simply become mythology and the Roman Bible would be the fact. The Romans commissioned the genocide of the Jews.

It didn't take long for the Jews to update their writings into monotheistic terms in the hopes that the Romans would retract the contract for their genocide. At this time the Jews initiated circumcisions so they would physically appear to be Romans. The Romans know that the Jews know too much. Better to exterminate them instead of risking being extorted or revealed at a later time.

The Genocide of the Jews, The Council of Nicaea and the Creation of the Roman Church was The Great Reset III.

If you had an issue with this or decided to ignore it and do your own thing, OFF WITH YOUR HEAD! The Roman Church would not tolerate your blasphemy.

At that time, the Romans were working on changing their appearance from vile slave masters to being your father. (After a short stint of OFF WITH YOUR HEAD).

Now you will now fall to your knees and kiss their feet when a Roman is near. He is the author of the Holy Roman Bible. The rule and guide to your morality and theology. They are your Fathers. They came from Heaven.

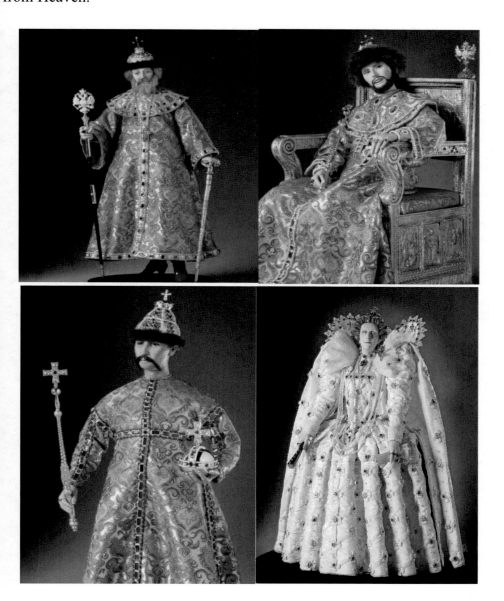

If Fauci, Gates and Schwaab's buddies wrote a new rule and guide for the theology and morality of all humans would you worship it? What if you would be canceled, fired, de-platformed or de-banked? What if they would chop off your head?

Romans subjugate humanity through religious manipulation.

V. Fake Fall of Rome

According to the historical accounts, A German King (Royal Roman) led the army that defeated Rome during the fake fall of Rome. Censor the Roman Empire so it never existed. No more Romans, no more Latin. No more slaves under boot, now humans are required to worship Roman Priests or be beheaded. Present the new Roman Bible to support the plan. Since Jews know the factual truth, exterminate them. Once they are gone, the Hebrew bible would become the myth and the Roman Bible would become the fact. A brutal but effective plan.

Here is the basic FAKE premise that we are supposed to believe. <u>The Roman Empire that appeared out of nowhere and dominated all of Europe and North Africa, the most advanced and powerful force that the Earth has ever witnessed has evaporated. Sixty million people stopped using Latin and now use the new languages created for their domains. The geniuses, scholars and scientists were accidentally murdered during the attack. All of it is just gone.</u>

Deleting the Roman civilization and the Latin language was the Great Reset IV.

This was not an accident, it was just another rewrite of history and a new form of human control.

It was a great reorganization of world religion.

Goodbye Roman Empire - Hello Roman church.

VI. Germany

In the most general terms, Germans were tribal until they were conquered by Romans. Then they became Christian based and very rapidly became the world's leader in technological advancements. Especially after they acquired the Roman scholars from the fake fall of Rome. Did all the Roman geniuses disappear? Did they accidentally murder them in battle? No, they captured them and took them back to the homeland like every victor of every war. This is another reason why Germany became so powerful and provided so many technological breakthroughs over the centuries.

These advancements were unleashed during WWI and WWII. Hilter was a Roman and his scientists were Romans. This is why he wanted to eradicate Jews and why he was so thirsty for power. He needed to build everything to the most colossal scale. Hitler was all about the purification of the Earth with the Master Race. Hitler was a slaver, wanted the Master Race in control, had access to advanced technology and faked his death. Hitler was born in a Roman Catholic family. **Hitler Was Clearly a Roman**.

The Italians *naturally being Romans* were all in with Hitler too. Depopulate the rapidly overcrowding Earth. This was only 70 years ago. ***WWI and WWII were the Great Reset V.***

VII. Russia

Romans had their own internal struggles for power. They split into eastern and western factions known as Eastern Orthodox (Russia) and Roman Catholics (Europe). The Eastern Roman Empire never really fell, but they do have struggles within. Eastern and Western Romans are at war today in Ukraine. Patriarch Kirill just threatened the end of the world forthcoming if any madmen were crazy enough to attack Russian soil. Russia has never lost a war. Now, in the year 2023, many other countries want to be part of the war, so they are sending advanced tanks and training to Ukraine. This is now a De facto World War. The doomsday clock has moved to 90 seconds to midnight. It doesn't look good for the planet Earth.

Patriarch Nikon Created a Schism among the Roman Orthodox

VIII. Big Tech

The Romans were the "big tech" back in the day and in total control. They are still the big tech today and still in total control. They don't stand in the open as GODS who have power over you, even though they are and they do. You will notice how the Romans and the human tools of the Romans are untouchable. They create their own (unelected) global economic forums and global governance forums. They simply *advise* world leaders who do as they are told.

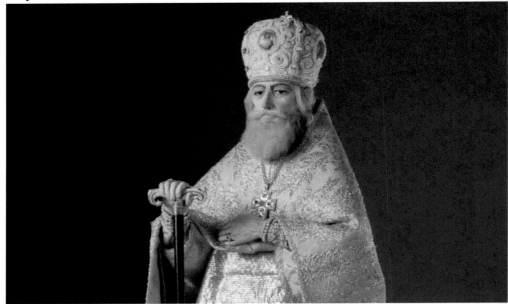

Romans - Patriarch Philaret

Humanity has purposefully been transitioned away from walking hand in hand with the Royal Romans. Humans were directed from worshiping the pantheon to worshiping one god and only getting to speak to the Middlemen. The Roman Priest. *Tell us your most sacred confessional secrets my child - I will forgive you.* This will cost you some money as your penance to GOD. (A well-designed manipulation to get you to admit your transgressions to your master). No need for that any more because they are big tech, they own all your passwords and accounts. They know your activities; they track and record your every move and conversation.

Confessional became obsolete once we had gmail, yahoo mail, iphones, location tracking, etc.

IX. Population Control

The world's population continues to explode unchecked. The Romans unleashed the virus that provided the means to restrict human rights and freedom. It created the invisible enemy to instill the fear required for the masses to surrender their most basic rights freely. They forced sterilizing spike shots on the masses while they enriched themselves. They censored effective existing treatments. They even enacted emergency authorizations to eliminate liability and corner the unwilling into submission. Emergency actions are on-going.

When your fish tank has too many snails, do you sterilize the snails? It seems like a nice way to clean up the mess. Mass murder is how it is usually accomplished. Let us be glad they are using sterilization techniques instead of mass murder.

If a spike shot causes sterilization, a heart attack or stroke, it is a lot nicer than outright mass murder. It is a lot neater and cleaner too. It is a gradual, slow-kill bioweapon.

Every form of sterilizing or killing humans has been enacted: Adult and child sex changes, physical attacks on food and energy sources, politically generated energy and food shortages through regulatory actions, monetary implosion, mass migrations, race wars, conventional wars, fentanyl epidemic, medical assisted suicide, fabricated pathogens and spike protein shots assist in the depopulation agenda. Enact censorship and force control through whatever means available, be it government mandate or a government recommended corporate mandate.

Now they are resetting the planet again. The phrase ***climate change*** is a code phrase for ***overpopulation***. This time there will be no god(s) to worship. You can now worship Anthony Fauci, the Spike Protein or the Global-Homo agenda. This will help keep the planet from overpopulating again so fast.

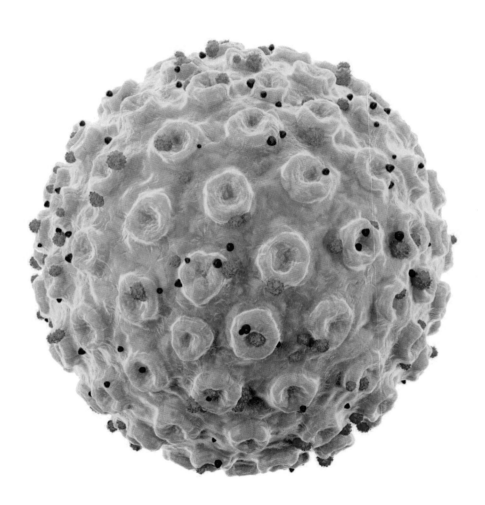

X. Great Reset

When you put a snail in your fish tank and six months later you have 300 snails, what do you do? You clean out the snails and start a fresh new tank. You might keep one snail even knowing what it will do. It will clean the bowl for you until it overpopulates. Then the fish bowl will need another great reset.

I am sorry to inform you that **we humans are the snails**. This is the Roman's world, it always has been. When they go on television and say they are executing a Great Reset, they are not talking to you and me, they are talking to the other Romans. If we can't control our population, then the Romans will. Children are the responsibility of the parent. They are our fathers, we are their children. The Earth is their fish tank, we are the snails.

Our Father who art in Heaven - get it yet?

When Klaus Schwaab announced *"I see the need for a great reset"* I knew something was amiss. Great Reset? Wipe the slate clean and start over? What bizarre language to use. In an instant, the entire globe was using the term *Great Reset*. It rapidly became clear that the Earth was under a global medical tyranny. Pathogens have been fabricated and released to accomplish a controlled biomedical takeover and sterilization agenda. Now I hear the Romans using the phrase *Build Back Better* (Globally). There should be no reason to build anything back because nothing has been torn down...

Now everything is being torn down... (Family, Gender, Morals, Energy, Food, Race, Borders, Currencies, Peace, Governments, Elections, etc...)

Here we are only 70 years since the last one and the Romans have initiated another *Great Reset*

Klaus Schwab has announced that in a few years you won't even recognize the Earth. It will be transformed into something greater. (A dumber human and a more controlling Roman master would be my guess - Serfs)

The release of pathogens, spike shot tyranny, fact checkers, mail in ballots, disinformation censors, de-platformers, de-bankers, tracers, ministry of truth, trackers, legal attacks, doxing, open borders, financial destruction and morality destruction is The Great Reset VI.

XI. Romans Today

There are Romans and there are tools of Romans.

The tools are the willing or unwilling, knowing or unknowing participants in the promotion of the Roman agenda. Most (like me and you) are simply caught in their intricate web of extortion.

The Romans and Roman tools are likely: Global Governance Forum, World Economic Forum, UN, WHO, Pope, DHS, Hollywood, CIA, Disney, Royals, Nazi, FBI, King Charles, Fauci, Big Tech, Gates, Zuckerberg, FDA, Deep-State, CDC, Hitler, Moderna, Big Media, Soros, Google, J.P. Morgan, Blackrock, Lagarde, Pfizer, Obama, Elites, Crime Families, Megacorps, Epstein, Governments, Globalist, NWO, and any other entity who wishes to control and destroy instead of supporting the freedom to choose one's own path.

Romans have humans intertwined with so many systems and methods of our extortion that we are all tools of the Romans in some form or fashion. The Romans have exploited humans at every level and opportunity from religion to banking and all things in between. They are above us on the food chain. We exist for their consumption as servants, labor and sex toys.

The looming questions are: Will the human races ever come together and overtake their masters? Is this why the Romans are sowing race division among the humans? Do they want to keep us fighting amongst ourselves so we will never have the time, initiative or ambition to question the subjects that have been discussed here?

Romans invented slavery and racism. Now they use it as a tool to generate infighting between the Earthly human races and to keep everyone distracted.

Back in the day, it was required for humans to confess their sins to their *Father*. Now they don't need you to confess your sins. They own your email accounts and all your passwords. (Google, Yahoo, Etc.,) They track your every movement. They own the security apparatus. You couldn't hide anything from them if you tried.

Would you rather be Pygmies, Eskimos, Aborigines or Indians? We actually would still be Neanderthals. Do you find it bizarre that we have ultra-advanced humans and yet we still have pockets of *natives*?

A *native* is simply a human who escaped Roman control.

There is one country on Earth where the slaves revolted, and the Romans walked away and let them have it. It is one of the most impoverished nations on the planet. If you're going to hate them, they might walk away. What would you have then, global Haiti? Roman rule might not be all that bad.

Belgium, Germany's neighbor is where many of them congregate now. They create their own world economic and global governance forums and simply take control of the planet through the WHO, UN, CDC and governments through sheer force of personality and other unseen manipulative actions.

XII. Anonymity

When one wants to disappear into the shadows so people stop looking for them (for any reason), what is the best way to disappear forever? *Fake your death.*

If you taught your slaves your mother tongue and wished it never happened, what would you do? *Confound languages and make the mother tongue a dead language.*

When your slaves don't know they are slaves, why would they revolt?

If you want to talk to your people exclusively while amongst others then you need your own language. The Latin mother tongue sure would be convenient since we already speak it. Let's get rid of Latin here on Earth so we can use it in underground communications and nobody will understand us. We can even speak it out in the open because if we do, people will just think we are Holy, because Latin is a Holy language.

These are the most basic reasons for the deletion of the roman empire and the roman language: If they don't exist, you cannot revolt against them. If it's a dead language then they won't understand us when we speak it.

Now that those **mean** Romans from the **mean** empire are gone you need to donate 10% of your income to the new **nice** Romans, **they are from heaven, they are your Fathers.** Nevermind the **off with your head** part. That was necessary to clear up any misinformation.

XIII. WITH Roman Influence

Who sprouted up out of the Earth with wildly advanced technology and all other aspects of a greatly advanced civilization? Skipping being natives altogether.

Who invented slavery and were the most vile slave masters ever?
Who impaled Christian humans, hung them on the end of a pole and burned
them at parties?

Romans - Emperor Nero.

Who worshiped a pantheon of gods for centuries and then suddenly worshiped a sole Christian GOD, created a new Roman church and expect you to kiss their feet and call them father.
Or else they will chop off your head.

Romans - Alexander VI

Leave 10% in the collection plate, my child. Remember, GOD is watching.

Who's planet is this?

Romans - Anastasia

Who are the authors of your rule and guide for all morality and religion?

Romans - King George III

Whose church has homosexual pedofiles and protects them?

Romans (Gilles de Retz - Known for violating young boys and murder)

Who owned the lands then, who owns the lands now?
Who was big tech then, who is big tech now?
Who owned religions then, who owns religions now?

Romans - Empress Catherine II

Who owns the media and promulgates all of the synchronous talking points?

Who created all of the social systems, laws and the disciplines of science that are used today?

Who owned the banks then, who owns the banks now?

Who are the puppet masters of the NSA, FBI, CIA, NSA, DHS, CDC, WHO, Federal reserve?

Who authored the Georgia guidestones?

Who is above the law?

Who is the New World Order?

Who is the Old World Order?

Who disappeared as mysteriously as they came?

The chimera myths from antiquity were not myths. They were trying to genetically enhance many different animals. It was a real horror show.

Solid evidence of genetic tampering - Cat or Dog?

XIV. WITHOUT Roman Influence

We would be 100% Neanderthals, not just 1% - 4%.
We *might* be advanced enough to make teepees, igloos and spears.
We would certainly not have COUNTLESS advances. **All advances, actually**. But most especially our genetics.

XV. Interesting Factoids

- One religion is particularly untouchable, owns their own sacred religious country (Vatican) and still speaks the *dead* mother tongue. It is wildly powerful. (Where exactly do they get their power?)

Marie DeMedici
Only a Roman would display themselves with such pomp.

- King Charles is on video stating that he is related to Vlad the Impaler.

- The all-seeing eye was a security camera.

- Belgium is a prime source of monkeypox because of the gay orgies.

- Brussels is the de-facto capital of Europe. (Romans really like it there - right next to their buddies in Germany too)

- There is a EuroNews debate series entitled: Brussels My Love.

- As Above - So Below. They are creating a colony that will be just like the mother planet. (Thy will be done on Earth as it is in Heaven, sound right?)

- Fauci is a natural born American from 1st generation Italian immigrants, possibly a pureblood Roman.

- The Romans landed in Kuwait, the great sphinx stares at the original landing site.

- They cut the face on a mountain on mars with the power beams from their ships to honor one of their kings who is buried in a cave under it. He was the very first Roman to visit Earth. His name was Alalu.

- Most edible plants come from the regions that the Romans originally frontiered.

- All Earthly primates have the rhesus gene. Yet 15% of humans have no rhesus factor in their blood (rh-).

- O- blood is universal to all other blood types and can donate to any of them. However an O- donor can ONLY accept O- blood. (Logically speaking this would mean that this blood would be from a genetic master bloodline, 7% of humans have this blood type)

- Negro Earthling humans are greatly superior as they grossly dominate any physical competition.

- There is no such thing as Satan/Lucifer. Just a boogeyman meant to scare children.

- When you encounter a person that makes predictions and they keep turning out to be correct then this person has been exposed to the existing advanced Roman culture. They are not prophetic or clairvoyant, they are simply stating how it is done on the homeworld. *Nostradamus, Leonardo da Vinci - thy will be done on Earth as it is in heaven and since this is how we do it in heaven I predict that this is how we will do it here on Earth.*

- The Great Pyramid was a lighthouse for spaceships. Its capstone was covered with electrum and was powered by crystals inside the structure. It emanated light in the four cardinal directions: North, South, East and West. This was the beacon for ships to align with for landing on Earth. At night, it lit the sky like daylight. Seen for many hundreds of miles in every direction it facilitated all Earthly navigation.

White people burn like vampires in sunlight. They are not from Earth.

Isabeau of Bavaria

XVI. They don't want you to go to Antarctica.

- Why did the Holy Roman Pope Francis go there?

- Why did Orthodox Roman Kirill go there?

- Why did Buzz Aldrin go there and what did he say upon his return?

- Why did Obama go there and then later send Biden there?

- Why did Hitler go there?

- Why is it such a secret place where all countries abide by a research treaty? No other place on Earth fosters such cooperation. Antarctica treaty of 1959 updated in 1991 makes it clear that they are protecting it in every possible way.

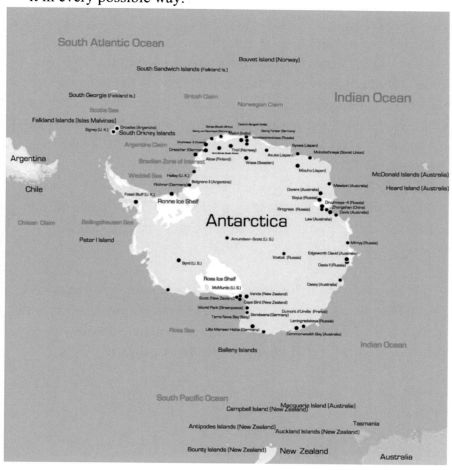

XVII. Epilogue

This book was intended to be very brief. It is too easy to get lost in the countless distractions and arguments that these subjects generate. I purposefully did not try to display cited facts or delineate timelines. Much of this information has been tainted over time. I am not trying to coerce or convince you of anything. I am simply telling you what happened. It is a high-level overview of the unfolding of the Earth being frontiered by Romans. You wondered who was behind the scenes as the puppet masters. Now you know. I would encourage you to investigate all facts presented.

Love them, hate them, worship them, fight them. You do you, but at the end of the day you actually have a lot to thank them for. **Every single thing, actually.**

The food of life and the water of life are the items that humans cannot obtain. These items are the reason why the Royal Romans can live 100 human lifetimes. They are not in the business of supplying these items to Earth, Earthlings were made to service them. They will never reveal their longevity. Shortened longevity keeps Earthlings in check. How wise and powerful can one get with a short lifespan? They will always fake their death and return at a later time as someone else or they will remain in the shadows.

If you think the evolutionary facts presented here are untrue, then you clearly believe that the Romans were super genius, brainiac X-men, naturally.

Elon shipped a car to his superiors when he launched a tesla into space, maybe they were going to evaluate his work and provide him with engineering details for his next models. Yes, rich people do crazy things as publicity stunts but nothing so insanely wasteful (as a test).

Ever seen a Negro or Asian Pope?
No, you never will.

Do modern Holy Romans want you to take spike shots?
Yes, mix them, match them and don't forget your boosters!

Do modern Holy Romans have a pedophile problem?
Yes, and they protect them.

Do all Romans have a pedophile problem?
Yes, they are protected. The FBI has Epstein's book of clients. Why have we not seen even one arrest of these perverts? You never will.

Why did Puritans flee to America? To escape religious persecution. In my humble opinion any religion that persecutes someone is not Holy. Religion should be voluntary and spontaneous or it is not authentic. Forced religion is absurd, it is slavery.

Satan/Lucifer/Hell is not real. This is a Roman construct. If you want a horse to pull a plow, offer it a carrot. If that doesn't work then beat it with a stick. Humans are controlled via the same premise. If you are good *you might* get to go to Heaven and live in eternal bliss OR if you are bad then *you will* go to Hell and suffer eternal damnation. This is the ultimate carrot and stick in concert. Better to be a good human. Make sure you give GOD 10%. He is all knowing.

I would challenge you to investigate for yourself to see how many people were decapitated or otherwise persecuted in the name of the Roman Church. Take a deep dive into the genetics of cheetahs as well.

Romans certainly deserve a level of respect and reverence for their contribution to humanity. I personally won't be worshiping, serving or paying them. They already get more than 50% of my income.

My agenda in writing this book was to help bring you out of the darkness and into the light. It took me 15 years of personal research to unravel these mysteries. I hope I have provided some real shortcuts for you in your delving into the Earth's actual past and what really happened. I am not trying to convince you of anything. If you already believe in something you go ahead and keep on believing it. I only tell you these things because they are true and real.

Thank you for taking the time to read and consider it.
Moose

Enjoy viewing these select items to add depth to your understanding:

History Channel - Ancient Top Ten; Rome's Greatest Hits S1E5, Ancient Greek Tech S1E7

YouTube - Zecharia Sitchin; Annunaki Lecture (forbidden-knowledge) 2:01:54

There were many images that I wished I could have used but I was unable to obtain permission.

I am not suicidal.

Made in the USA
Las Vegas, NV
25 February 2023

68125914R00036